Lose Your STRESS, Find Your JOY!

Lose Your Stress, Find Your Joy!

Lisa Creedon

ଙ୍କଃ

Alcovy Press
www.alcovypress.com

Published by
Alcovy Press
2001_108

Copyright 2011, 2015 by Lisa Creedon

All rights reserved. No part of this publication may be reproduced or transmitted in any form or by any means, electronic or mechanical, including photocopy, recording, or any information storage and retrieval system, without permission in writing from the copyright owner.

ISBN: 978-0-9833039-1-6

Library of Congress Control Number: 2011916541

Printed in the United States of America.

Disclaimer and Terms of Use: No information contained in this book should be considered as financial, tax, legal or medical advice. Usage of information and content obtained by you at or through this publication is solely at your own risk. Alcovy Press or the author assume no liability or responsibility for damage or injury to you, other persons, or property arising from any use of any product, information, idea, or instruction contained in the content or services provided through this book. The author has no financial interest in nor receives any compensation from manufacturers of products or websites mentioned in this book. Neither the publisher nor the author assumes any responsibility for third-party websites or their content.

*To Lindsay and Leslie,
my greatest joys!*

Contents

1. "If it is to be, it's up to me" 1
   Anne's Story 2
   The Search for Joy 3
   When Something Steals our Joy 4
   Choosing to be Happy 5
   Our Inner Voice 8
   The Power of Words & Thoughts 8
2. Is it Just Bad Luck? 13
   What Is Free Will? 15
   Everybody Makes Mistakes 19
   Anger 20
   Forgiveness 20
3. The Basics 23
   The Right Fuel 24
   A Good Night's Sleep 26
   Emotional Needs 27
   Just Say No 29
   Givers and Takers 30
   Needs and Wants 31
   If Only…. 31
4. Curses and Blessings 33
   The Curse of Critical People 33
   The Curse of Emotional Needy People 35
   The Curse of Being a Martyr 36
   The Curse of Bitterness 38
   The Curse of Food and Drink 39
   You Can Change It 41

5.	Personal Value	43
	Friendly Beginnings	43
	Relationship Woes	44
	Compliments & Conversation	45
	Children Need Respect, Too	46
	Turn It Around	46
6.	Find Your Joy!	49
Study Guide		63

Acknowledgements

Friends and personal events inspired me to write this book. I hope it will provide the inspiration and motivation you need to find your joy each and every day!

For their expertise, advice and proofing, many thanks to Ellen Minton and Tony Socci.

With much appreciation for their encouragement and moral support, I want to thank Lindsay Prather, Leslie Creedon, Dr. Cindy Bristow, Barbara Cone, Stan Davis, Cille Allen, Suzanne Lunsford, and Carol McDonough.

I also want to thank my family for their willingness, patience, enthusiasm, and opinions each time I asked, "What do you think about this?"

*Find out where joy
resides, and give it
a voice far
beyond singing.
For to miss joy
is to miss all.*

– *Robert Louis Stevenson*

Chapter One
"If it is to be, it's up to me"
— *Author Unknown*

If it is to be, it's up to me. What a great quote! It really covers everything, for we are ultimately responsible for our own well-being – mental and physical. Regardless of how inept we might feel at times, we are directly in control of how we handle the various challenges that come our way. As we look at how stress affects our joy in this book, *it's up to me* will be a constant theme.

For many of us, the greatest challenge we face each day is how high our stress level will be. Will traffic problems start our day and take us to the breaking point before 9 a.m.? Will our already stressful workload or workplace conditions send our blood pressure soaring? Do we reach our breaking point when interacting with our spouse or children or other situations in our homes?

Through almost daily articles, new reports tell us that stress is directly responsible for many of today's medical conditions. Stress affects all of the basics, such as our blood pressure, weight and sleep, but it also affects our total being.

More than just an emotional strain, stress affects us physically. People faced with constant stress can experience such visible signs as extreme hair loss and various outbreaks (hives, rashes, etc.), but stress can also affect us internally. Ulcers, colitis, and other ailments are common examples, but the effects of stress are now known to run much deeper.

Anne's Story

"Anne" found herself suddenly disabled by a severe pain and swelling in her left leg. Walking was difficult, and she spent many hours on the sofa with ice packs on her elevated leg. Her knee was very swollen.

Since there was no apparent injury, doctors were mystified and refused to drain the fluid from her knee because "there was damage and the fluid would simply return." The diagnosis she received was probable rheumatoid arthritis with a suggestion for extensive additional testing.

The pain and swelling began the day after her father suddenly passed away. She traveled out of town to make arrangements and was surprised when her leg became painful and swollen.

Assuming she had somehow twisted her knee or pulled a muscle, she limped through the funeral, the initial phase of filing the Will, and preparing the house for sale.

Two months later, with her leg still swollen and her knee in pain, she again traveled to meet with attorneys to finalize the sale of the house. On her way home, she met with a trusted chiropractor friend about her leg. Convinced he would identify the problem, Anne was even more puzzled when he found nothing wrong.

A short time later, the pain and swelling disappeared as suddenly as it had come. It was a mystery.

Months later with the occurrence of another highly stressful event, the knee pain and swelling recurred in a matter of hours. Anne then realized the problem was caused totally by stress.

With the second occurrence, Anne took immediate action to relieve her stress level through prayer (to find the support, peace, and joy she was missing), exercise, and this time, confrontation and resolution with the person who was responsible for the stress attack. The pain and swelling quickly disappeared. Her actions were a great example of *if it is to be, it's up to me*.

The Search for Joy

Anne's story is far from unusual. While doctors know stress is damaging, traditional medicine too often still tries to treat symptoms rather than looking for the cause of the problem.

Doctors might prescribe antidepressants for stress, and the pills might help; however, if the stress is due to an ongoing situation in your life, pills generally will not resolve the problem that is causing the stress.

The search for joy, for happiness, for a stress-free environment, is a hot topic these days. It is rather sad, in this time of technological wonders, that one of our basic needs can seem so elusive. Even our founding fathers, as they struggled to create our *Declaration of Independence*, knew the "pursuit of happiness" was of primary importance.

When we are stress free, we have joy. We feel better. We feel healthier, smarter. There is a bounce in our step. Our shoulders are back and our heads are held a little higher. We greet challenges with confidence.

That is where we *want* to be and where we *need* to be. Happy people have fewer health problems because their days are not filled with stress and worry. And they generally have fewer relationship problems. Why? Because happy people attract more joy into their lives!

When Something Steals Our Joy

Have you ever heard that true happiness comes from within? That we are responsible for our state of happiness?

Basically, yes, we are responsible for our state of happiness; however, sometimes it is not as simple as choosing joy or sadness. Often, there are gray areas that directly affect our ability to experience joy.

For example, you might have been happier before your health failed, before the car wreck that left you disabled, before your spouse died, before your job was eliminated – certainly stressful situations.

Or perhaps stress overcame your joy through arguments with your spouse or best friend, problems with your children, financial problems, or any number of other joy-stealers.

For many of us, every day is not going to be a perfect day. When stressful times occur, we must realize:

Everyone has challenges; we are not in this alone.

We must be kind to ourselves, just as we are kind to others.

Everyone has to throw a pity party at some point, just don't stay at the party.

On a particularly bad day when we are more emotional than usual, when nothing seems to be going right, when we are tempted to throw up our hands and dramatically exclaim, "All hope is lost!", that is when we should step back and draw upon a much-used scriptural phrase: *and it came to pass.* This portion of a verse is found 396 times in the King James Bible, 62 times in Genesis.

If we look at a problem in that light, that *it came to pass – it did not come to stay*, we can experience instant relief. Most of our problems do not come to stay; however, it is our responsibility to look for the positive aspects of the situation and for viable solutions.

When we experience problems, or if we are simply feeling down and out, we cannot give in to those *temporary* situations. Life is continually changing. We must look for answers, for the solution that can change our outlook – and perhaps our life.

Choosing to be Happy

For some of us, joy is like a beautiful butterfly flitting about, sometimes landing on our shoulder, often fluttering teasingly just beyond our reach. If we chase the butterfly, it may fly faster or higher to escape. And so goes our search for joy.

Every day, we can choose to be happy or sad. We can choose to find the positive part of a situation or to be negative and critical. While it is always possible for negativity to creep in and steal our joy, we know that approaching a bad situation with negative thoughts does not fix anything and actually makes us feel even worse.

Sometimes family members or others who are close to us can be the biggest joy-stealers of all. If that is a problem in your life, make time to sit and talk about it – one on one with that person.

Angry people are often unhappy or frustrated. What seems to be a large problem could be resolved by simply addressing a misunderstanding. People may not know the anguish they are causing and might be relieved for the opportunity to make a relationship better.

When circumstances steal our joy, we need to think about how we are responding to a particular situation. Getting upset or angry does nothing to resolve the problem.

Let's say you have an important appointment and are running behind schedule in leaving your house. Even worse, now you cannot find your car keys. Your blood pressure rises as you frantically search for the keys. Where is the joy in this situation?

Realize this might be your destiny, or you might say God is watching over you. If you had left at the planned moment, perhaps you would have been in worse traffic, possibly a car accident. In other words, it might have been very important that you did not leave exactly when you planned.

Take a deep breath and, out loud, retrace your steps from when you last saw your keys. Frantic yelling at family members does nothing but make everyone more upset. Approaching challenges with a peaceful attitude can save much frustration and bad feelings.

Perhaps a friend or family member does not seem to be listening or caring when we try to talk. Rather than going immediately to anger, ask that person if there is a problem

Step back and think about what might be going on in their life, something that might make them less concerned about what you are saying.

Sometimes you must realize there are people who simply care more about themselves than they do about others. Accepting this fact can be aggravating; however, look for the peace in knowing the person is not rejecting *you*, that is just how they are.

If it is to be, it's up to me. Don't let go of your joy, and don't give in to stress or anger. Be thoughtful and considerate of others; it will come back to you.

Sometimes, we must consciously stop and find our peace. And sometimes, we just need to give our inner voice a chance to speak. Many issues can be avoided when we listen to that quiet voice.

Our Inner Voice

Each of us has an inner voice; however, many choose not to listen. Because the voice is quiet, some claim not to hear it.

What is this inner voice? If we are spiritual, we may believe the voice to be God, Jesus, or the Holy Spirit. Some believe the voice is their Guardian Angel.

Some say it is our conscience but regardless what you believe, our inner voice is important and can help us avoid many problems if we listen.

Our inner voice is always there, working day and night, trying to guide us through life. The voice is always quiet, always gentle as it urges us to do something (or not do something) – to make the right choice.

Problems frequently arise from ignoring what the inner voice is telling us to do. Our inner voice is only interested in what is best for us; it will never intentionally direct us toward the wrong path.

The Power of Words & Thoughts

Does it sometimes seem that every day is just another set of challenges? Can you remember the last time you really laughed and enjoyed yourself? Are you barely making it through each day with your burdens of worry and stress?

When periods of struggle arise, what do you do? Do you worry constantly? Do you keep repeating, "What am I going to do? All I have is bad luck!"

Stop for a moment and think about your focus. When we are upset, too often our focus is on being upset, rather than on resolving our problem.

To make positive changes, we must focus on positive thoughts. Even a significant problem could be the beginning of a positive change in our life.

Years ago when computer programming was just taking off, "Dave" became a paraplegic after a bad dive into a pool. Not content to be bored and throw pity parties, he discovered he had excellent computer skills and developed a successful computer business. *If it is to be, it's up to me.*

Our words and thoughts are powerful and have a direct reflection on our inner being. If we speak negative words and think negative thoughts, that is, if we continue to talk about our problems and stay consumed with worry, we risk sinking deeper and deeper into a pit of despair.

If you are a chronic worrier, answer this question: *Has worrying about a problem ever made a difference in the outcome?* Truly, worry in itself does not solve any problem. It can, however, keep you stressed and depressed.

If you have developed the habit of speaking negatively about yourself or your situation, stop that right now! Everyone has an off day now and then, but no one should be beating themselves up daily with comments like, "I must be stupid. What's wrong with me? Why do bad things happen to me all the time?"

Just as negative thoughts can drag us into more negative situations, positive thoughts have the reverse effect.

To put yourself in a more positive frame of mind, try using some of these positive affirmations:

I love and approve of myself.

Things happen. I know everything will work out okay.

I forgive myself for whatever mistakes I have made.

I may not understand why this happened, but I know all will work out the best possible way.

I will not allow anger to control me.

I believe in my abilities and know I work hard.

I will not allow fears and worries to drain my energy.

My past has no power over me.

If things are not working out the way I want, I will change what needs to be changed..

We can control some things, but we cannot control everything. It is important to identify the things we *can* control and to develop positive thoughts about how to work with our challenges.

If you are experiencing challenges right now, sit back, take a deep breath and take the time to acknowledge all of the positives in your life. Can you see, hear, talk, or walk? Those are blessings everyone does not have. When we lose our joy, sometimes we need to stop and count our blessings.

Regardless of current challenges, we can always find something positive. There is an old saying: "every dark cloud has a silver lining." Even when things look bleak, everything in our life is not bad.

Sometimes we have to take a deep breath and make a conscious decision to find the good – to find our joy.

Try this Experiment:

Out loud, say, "Oh my gosh!" "What can I do? What is going to happen?!" Repeat it several times. Say it anxiously while you are thinking of a bad situation. Can you feel yourself becoming more anxious?

Now, speak calmly: "Things are going to improve. I know everything will work out for the best. I am at peace." And *believe* it. Can you feel yourself taking a deeper breath and becoming more relaxed?

When we focus on negative things, we stay in a frantic state of mind. This does not allow us to work toward a positive solution.

While we might be seeking a fast, physical answer (immediate cash, job, place to live, etc.), we are also seeking happiness within ourselves and a sense of peace. It is a lot easier to find an answer when we are working from a base of peace.

Let's take a moment to look at things we should *not* do, things that can hold us back:

What Not To Do

- ***Do not waste time trying to find someone or something to blame.***
- ***Do not speak negatively about yourself.***
- ***Do not wallow in "if only" thinking.***

Blaming other people or situations will accomplish two main things:

(1) we will remain bitter, and
(2) our creativity to resolve the problem and move forward can be blocked. Until we can think clearly, we may not be able to identify the root of our problem.

Sometimes it is hard not to blame. We may feel that parents or a spouse failed us, and it might be true. Our parents or spouse may have been harsh instead of loving, might have said no instead of offering support at a crucial time. Our grown child might have made decisions that adversely affected the entire family.

There are many situations, some worse than others, that have shaped our lives; however, we cannot stay immersed in self-pity and continue to blame others for our perceived misfortune. That attitude will not change anything. Joy is still out there, even if you have to jump a few hurdles to reach it!

Many times, our problems are caused by decisions *we* have made. To move forward, we must take responsibility for past decisions and decide how we can change the situation, maybe change our future.

Chapter Two

Is It Just Bad Luck?

Some people get stuck in the idea that they are just unlucky, that they were dealt a bad hand in the game of life. Whether their parents were rich or poor, attentive or absent, these folks have a list of excuses as to why they have a bad life. Worse, many think God has either forgotten them or that he is deliberately making them suffer.

God gave us free will, and that gives us the right to make choices. You can believe in God or you can believe in luck, but you cannot believe in both.

God's intention was that we choose to love him and honor him by making good choices in life. However, free will also allows us to make choices that are not good. When that happens, we must take responsibility for those decisions without blaming God, others, or bad luck. The only way to resolve our problem is to take responsibility for our decision and examine all possible solutions.

For example, if we are sick, possibly with a serious disease, we must look at how we are living. Here are a few things that can lead to better health:

Eating healthy foods (no fast food or processed food)

Drinking enough water and choosing the right drinks (no colas, no high fructose corn syrup)

Getting enough sleep

Exercising regularly

Actively trying to reduce our stress level

Not smoking

When necessary, seeing a medical practitioner who looks for the cause of an illness rather than simply treating symptoms

Many problems/bad luck come from our own, willful, bad decisions. If we refuse to take responsibility for problems arising from our bad decisions, we cannot find happiness while we busily seek someone or something to blame.

Unless we take responsibility for our actions, we will continue to experience problems – possibly the same ones – over and over again. Some people choose to blame God for everything that goes wrong in their lives. But is he really to blame?

Is it God?

Some people believe God directs our every step and that every single action is directly from him. I, too, believe in a Master Plan; however, *free will* seems to keep jumping in there and messing things up.

The Bible actually does not use the words *free will*. Instead, there are references throughout where people *chose* to follow their own path rather than the one God wanted them to follow.

For example, Eve *chose* to eat the apple, and Adam *chose* to eat it also. Cain *chose* to kill Abel. Jonah *chose* to run from God. Saul *chose* to persecute Christians. Sampson *chose* to give into Delilah.

Are there times in your life where you have chosen the wrong path, knowing it was probably not the best decision? Did you blame yourself? Did you blame someone else? Did you blame God?

Here are some examples:

If there is an unplanned pregnancy, is that bad luck? Is it a gift or curse from God? Is it because someone made a bad choice and did not consider the consequences?

If people are always making you angry and you seem to go from one bad situation to the next, is it really your bad luck? Is God constantly putting the wrong people in your path? Do you really think it is everyone else? Are you willing to accept that you might need to work on some personal issues?

If your car quits, is it bad luck? Does God "just have it in for you?" Or could it be because you did not take care of your car?

If you hate your job or need things your employer does not provide, is that really just bad luck? Is it the fault of the Almighty Creator? Of course not. You should look for a new job or possibly a new career.

> If you need better pay or better hours, health insurance or a less stressful environment, don't get mired down in critical thinking or hopelessness. Talk to more people; get involved in groups where you might learn about different areas of interest or new opportunities.

> Do you need better computer skills to get a job? Goodwill Industries offers free computer training at _www.gcflearnfree.org_. Another great site that offers free and pay-for training videos is _www.lynda.com_. Also, instructional videos can be found on youtube.com on just about any topic.

If you are miserable in your marriage and blaming God, did you even consult him before you married that person? Instead of blaming, get counseling. Yes, that can be expensive but not nearly as costly as a divorce. Look for counseling services that have sliding fee scales or check with larger churches to see if they offer in-house marital counseling.

Is your child is out of control? That has nothing to do with luck or God. The general thought is that children are not born "bad." Get counseling. It is too easy for a family to be torn apart. Learn how to make a difference for your child and for yourself, and be open to making changes.

Did God want that person to develop cancer or some other dreaded disease? Of course not. In the Bible, we are told what to eat. If we *choose* a diet of fast food, restaurant food, junk food and processed foods full of chemicals, our bodies will respond accordingly.

Did you notice a pattern in those examples? In each one, the problem and solution involve very human decisions. It is not luck or fate or God. When we stop blaming and accept responsibility for the choices we have made, we can begin to make improvements in our life. We can begin to heal.

Here is another example: You fell and broke your arm or leg. Was it God? Was it bad luck? "Doesn't God know I need to drive?" or "Doesn't God know I can't work now?"

Don't think about blame, and don't spend time and energy worrying about something you cannot fix. Don't think about what you *cannot* do; use your energy to think about what you *can* do – changes you need to make to work around this challenge.

What about prayer? Does this mean we don't pray? Of course not. We should always pray. The combination of prayer and positive thinking is vitally important. However, if you have no job and no money, prayer and positive thinking in itself will not change anything.

If you pray 24 hours a day for a job but never submit an application or resume, your chances of getting a job are pretty slim. Pray, think positive thoughts, update your resume, and actively pursue your goal.

Regardless of what you are wanting and praying about, positive thinking and "doing something about it" generally make the difference.

Sometimes things happen that force us to make changes in our lives. Death is probably the biggest change. Some people get angry at God when a loved one dies. While they are praying, *"Thy will be done,"* they are actually thinking, "But this is what *I* want."

Losing someone you love, whether person or treasured pet, is the one of the most difficult pains we bear. But as true believers, we must accept God's will in all things.

When my horse was sick, I prayed mightily for his recovery. I felt God could cure him, and we certainly were ill-prepared for the unexpected $1,000 vet bill. Five years later, I still mourn losing him and still do not understand why he had to go. But I accept that this had to happen – for reasons I cannot understand.

Sometimes *we* force things to happen. Perhaps we do not have a good feeling about the situation. Maybe there are warning signs that continuing with a particular decision is a bad choice, and yet we forge ahead.

When there are warning signs or if you feel uneasy about a certain decision, consider all options before continuing. If you choose to ignore the signs and feelings, there are often negative consequences.

In my family, we have a rule that we pay attention to the circumstances involving a major decision. If odd things continue to happen (signs) and there is a feeling of uneasiness about the situation, we accept that this particular decision might not be the right one. We believe having peace about the decision is the best indicator that it is the right decision.

God is not petty. He does not watch for opportunities to smack us (even if we need it). He gave us *free will* to be responsible for our decisions. We cannot blame him for our lack of attention to what is going on around us or for bad decisions we make without consulting him properly.

God's primary concern is our eternal salvation. He wants us to read the Bible and spend time with him in prayer. We are to seek his will and purpose for our lives. He is also there to help us make decisions when we consult him and give him a chance to answer.

Everybody Makes Mistakes

Everyone has made mistakes. Even if it wasn't a huge mistake, most people can quickly recall at least one big goof in life where they would like to have a "do over."

Of course, we cannot go back in time and have that opportunity, so there is nothing to be gained by continuing to rehash what could have/should have been. Let it go.

Anger

At some point in life, many people have felt deep anger. If you are angry with a person – or perhaps a doctor or a company – so angry that you actually feel hate, it can fill your life with stress and continual unhappiness as you replay the situation over and over in your mind. It steals your joy, perhaps on a daily basis.

Sometimes we feel we have been wronged and lash out in anger. But even if we were intentionally wronged, we must reach some type of resolution and move on.

Anger affects you, not the person at whom you are angry. Sure, you can act mean or be silent with your spouse, friend or child and yes, you will hurt them. But the anger boiling inside of you is much more destructive. Also, your anger or wrath will not resolve the problem, it will steal your joy.

Perhaps a store clerk was rude or a driver cut you off in traffic. Are you going to let one bad moment ruin your day? Take a deep breath, think of pleasant things, and move on.

We can only control so many things, certainly not everything. We must resolve issues as best we can, put them behind us, and find our joy.

Forgiveness

If you need to forgive someone, do that now. Forgiveness does not mean you must like the person or welcome them into your home.

To regain your joy, you must make peace with whatever happened, hopefully by resolving it with the person (or company) to the best of your ability, then forget it and move on. Free your mind of that stress.

An old saying is "Don't cry over spilt milk." That means the milk has already been spilled on the floor and there is no way to recover it.

Continuing to bash yourself or others will not save the milk, so it is best to find your peace, "clean up the mess," realize this was just a minor setback in the scheme of things, and regain your joy!

Regardless of what "milk" has spilled, fussing and arguing about who or what was at fault cannot change anything. It only makes the situation more stressful and keeps the negative energy flowing.

To move forward and make positive changes, we should examine all possible solutions, find our peace, and be willing to take responsibility for our decisions.

The important thing is to regain your joy by letting go of any emotional baggage so you can get back to more important issues.

~ If it is to be, it's up to me. ~
The only way to overcome a problem is to take responsibility for your decision and examine all possible solutions.

Chapter Three
The Basics

On our journey to lose stress and find joy, we must consider our physical and emotional needs. It is more difficult to be joyful and make good decisions when you are so tired you can hardly see straight and are consuming large amounts of caffeine just to keep going.

Proper food and adequate rest are basic needs and are especially important during stressful times. Healthy food choices keep our bodies at optimum running capacity.

Stress depletes Vitamins B and C from our bodies and affects other vitamin and mineral levels. Eating healthy during stressful times is very important; however, supplements may be necessary.

Check with your doctor for issues of concern. You might want to consider a doctor who prefers natural remedies over prescription medications.

There is a lot of health information online. You might want to consider info from www.drjoelfuhrman.com and www.mercola.com. Both of these sites share information on a large number of topics and promote a healthy lifestyle.

My feeling is "nobody knows everything." No human being can know absolutely everything there is to know, including doctors. The Internet is a valuable source to find out what you need to know about eating healthy foods. It is best to always check your information with more than one source.

A Good Night's Sleep

An adequate amount of quality sleep is vital, especially during stressful times. Sleep-deprived people frequently end up eating more food, and craving non-healthy foods, as they attempt to give their bodies enough fuel to make it through the day.

If sleep problems are an issue, try these suggestions:

- Eliminate caffeine of any type including soda and chocolate. Decaffeinated tea still has a bit of caffeine and can be enough to keep some people awake.

- Set an earlier bedtime and stick to it. If you have trouble falling asleep, give your body time to adapt to your new schedule. Read until you are tired rather than watching television.

- Two hours before bedtime, do not use the computer or do anything else that stimulates your brain. Also, the light from the computer, television, or smart phone can cue your body that it is time to wake up.

- Keep paper beside your bed and list any concerns you are afraid you might not remember later.

- Don't nap in the late afternoon or early evening.

- Earlier in the day, walking or other exercise can help your body be more tired and ready for sleep at night.

- Do not eat or drink anything except water two hours before going to bed.

- If you get too warm at night, try sheets and blankets made of 100% cotton instead of polyester blends. If your head is hot, try a cotton pillowcase on a feather pillow. Polyester holds heat.

- Do not watch action-packed, scary or violent movies or get involved in heated conversations right before bedtime. To put a baby to bed, we rock, read and sing in a dimly lit room. Just as that helps a baby sleep, you also need to relax and wind down so you can peacefully drift off to sleep.

- Review good things that happened that day or tell yourself a familiar story *(see page 55 for details)*.

The Right Fuel

Just like our cars need good gasoline and quality parts, our bodies need the right fuel to run properly. Without the right fuel, our health and energy levels sputter and spark.

Instead of making healthy choices, some folks try to get by with high-caffeine energy drinks and the small, expensive packs of "super energy" vitamins sold on convenience store counters.

While we probably know people who live almost solely on pizza and other fast food, most of us know the right foods to eat to promote good health and prevent future problems.

Basics include palm-sized portions of meat (or other protein), limited quantities of carbohydrates, lots of fresh veggies and salads, some fruit, and lots of water.

We probably know to stay away from white breads and sugar. As this is not an in-depth health article, we won't go into the high fructose corn syrup issue and other bad choices.

Eating healthy food (plus exercise) is our best defense against a variety of health problems. Major illnesses are often the result of unhealthy diets.

While almost everyone must fulfill a chocolate craving from time to time, we need to keep the big picture in mind: our joy and energy levels are closely tied to our health.

What about "comfort foods?" While a bag of potato chips or chocolate chip cookies might seem immediately comforting, those items also deliver a truckload of guilt through calories along with a temporary carbohydrate or sugar high.

Worse, those foods make you want to consume even more of that type food. Colas, for example, whether diet or regular, make you crave the wrong foods. Whoever heard of eating fresh veggies with a nice cold can of Coke? Why do you think fast food meals include sodas?

A better, more comforting choice is homemade chicken soup (store bought works, too), a bowl of spaghetti, lasagna, chili – you get the idea.

If weight is a stress point for you, check out "Eat to Live" by Dr. Joel Fuhrman. Not only does his book offer a great diet, but the success stories of people who have been healed of many serious diseases *just through diet* are very impressive.

De-stressing: For some, a cup of hot tea or coffee is a great way to relax the body and mind. Sometimes it is a matter of getting away from the stressful situation by taking a walk or sitting somewhere else for a short time. A change of scenery can work wonders. "Take a Break" is great advice any time stress is involved!

> You can't change the past, but you can ruin the present by worrying over the future.
> ~Anonymous

Emotional Needs

Of equal or perhaps greater importance to our physical needs are our emotional needs. When our emotions get the best of us, when we no longer feel we can see a light at the end of the tunnel, that is when everything starts to unravel. To keep from plummeting into the depths of despair, we need these things:

Hope. Without hope, we are powerless. In challenging times, we must believe things can change for the better. Thankfully, most of us will never know a life that is truly without hope. Regardless of how bad things might get, it is human nature to remain hopeful as we count our current blessings and plan for better days ahead.

Love. Whether from our significant others, children, family members, parents, friends or our special pets, we cannot exist without love in our lives. Always make time to let the ones you love know how you feel.

Care. Love and care are closely related; however, even if there is no major source of love in our lives, we can get by if we know there are people who genuinely care for us.

"The biggest disease this day and age is that of people feeling unloved." ~ Diana, Princess of Wales.

Take time to reach out to others. As our lives become more intertwined with computers, there is less human involvement than ever before. Sometimes the best way to combat loneliness is to help others. *See page 57 for more information about loneliness.*

Faith. While faith and hope are similar in definition, the dictionary makes an important distinction: hope is the feeling that what is wanted can be had. Faith, however, is defined as a belief or a confidence (in a person or thing).

Faith in God is a uniting factor among believers, and that strong faith sustains them through tough times. If you are strong in your faith, you cannot be consumed with worry.

Just Say No

Some people look to others or to material things for happiness. Honestly, no one else (and no material object) has the power to create joy if that person is otherwise miserable.

While a miserable person might be temporarily distracted by someone or something, the misery will quickly return once the distraction is over. Worse, people who are miserable generally try to make others feel guilty for not providing a continuing source of entertainment/happiness.

> Learn to say no.
> Remember, "yes"
> rhymes with stress!

When we allow certain people or situations to make us unhappy, it can be because we do not feel we are important enough to stand up to that person or situation. Know that we are all equally important and that your happiness is just as important as anyone else's – for your mind and especially for your health.

A famous quote by Eleanor Roosevelt is good to remember: *No one can make you feel inferior without your consent.* And to take that a step further, no one can make you *do* anything without your consent.

Sometimes we must learn to say "No." If you have a problem saying No, try saying, "I'm sorry, I just can't do that right now" or "I'm sorry, I have already made other plans." If the person is too persistent, you could say, "I'm sorry, I just don't feel like doing that now." Remember, "yes" rhymes with stress!

Givers and Takers

Some folks are "Givers" by nature. Giving gives them joy. They willingly give away their time, their money, their material goods, maybe even space in their homes. And then there are the "Takers". Takers are generally pretty good at finding Givers. Once a Taker has exhausted a Giver, the Taker simply moves on to find another Giver.

Givers should be cautious and set boundaries for the Taker -- because Takers do not have any boundaries. Many Takers will happily take your last dime and think bad of you because you had no more to offer.

There is great joy in giving to others – but sometimes you have to know when to say "No".

Needs and Wants

Sometimes we lose our joy when our *needs* get confused with our *wants*. The key word is *need*. We know that needs are different from wants. If we aren't careful, a bad case of *wants* can steal our joy.

One example would be cars. While we might *want* a brand new, super deluxe vehicle that would impress both friends and strangers, do we really *need* to struggle to make high monthly payments for the next six or more years plus paying higher insurance fees? Money is often closely tied to needs and wants, and we must be careful not to let money steal our joy.

Our *wants* are sometimes fed by charge cards. If we are already experiencing problems with debt, we must resist the temptation to accommodate our wants.

For our needs, we should try to save until we can pay cash and, when possible, not use credit cards for routine purchases. Increasing our debt and monthly payments can also increase our stress level and steal our joy.

If Only....

Some folks have a bad case of the "If only's..." If only I were married, if only I were single, if only I had a better job, if only my spouse had a better job, if only I had a better car or house, if only my kids were older (or younger, or more respectful) and, of course, if only I had more money.

While some of those things might bring temporary happiness, the only true happiness comes from inner peace.

When we depend on others or have conditions for our joy, we are often disappointed.

If you are having trouble finding happiness, get a pen and some paper. On the first page, list the things that currently bring you joy.

This could also be considered a "count your blessings" list and include such things as good health, positive people in your life, and material things such as your home and other possessions.

On the next page, list things you *think* would bring you joy. Seeing a list on paper helps gives clarity to our thoughts. If some of the items listed are real goals you could pursue, follow up on them.

For example, losing weight or developing an exercise program might be on that page. List ways you might achieve that goal. Maybe you would be happier with a different job – or perhaps you want to make a career move. Research your options, decide which goals are realistic, list ways to achieve them, and get to work on making your goal a reality.

Most people get great satisfaction from doing something they are proud of, something that requires an effort. Choose wisely. If "win the lottery" is on your list, that might not be the most realistic goal. Worse, the only way to achieve that goal would be to spend even more money buying lottery tickets.

Confront problem areas in your life and make decisions that will create a positive direction and help you find your joy.

CHAPTER FOUR

Curses and Blessings

The Curse of Critical People.

People who criticize others are basically energy vampires. If we are feeling great and encounter an energy vampire, we may leave (the visit, meeting, phone call, etc.) feeling totally drained. Critical people can steal our joy.

Sometimes critical people don't attack us directly. They might tell stories about others, but we realize later that the story was directed toward us.

Or perhaps they are not directly critical of us, but they can't seem to say anything positive about anyone or anything. This leads us to wonder what they say behind our back. Either way, it is exhausting to listen to someone who constantly complains.

While the first inclination for many of us is to try to help people in need, we must realize that:

> (1) they cannot be helped unless they actually *want* help (some do not want help; they just want to complain and have someone listen), and

> (2) many times, they do not realize the problem lies within themselves; instead, they blame others for everything.

It is difficult to be around critical people. Sometimes it is effective to change the subject or refuse to participate when the criticizing begins.

Especially if we have our own problems, it may be best to try to avoid persistently critical folks. However, that can be difficult if the person is a member of our family.

When a family member is causing undue stress, we might not be able to end that relationship, but it is perfectly fine to tell the person their comments make us unhappy. That does not mean they will change, but it is important to be gently assertive for our own sanity.

Find the Blessing

Everyone needs to vent their frustrations from time to time, but constantly dwelling on problems is depressing.

When we are faced with daily stress, particularly if we are providing care for family members, it is important to find other people (or other outlets) that will be a blessing to us and help us find joy.

Associate with people who have a positive outlook and are doing interesting things. Talk with someone who has a great sense of humor and makes you laugh.

Laughter and exercise are powerful weapons against stress. A good laugh or workout (even a nice walk) can clear your mind, change your outlook, and help you deal with frustrating circumstances.

The Curse of Emotionally Needy People.

This curse is similar to the previous one and drains your energy just as quickly. Once a needy person latches on, they will drain your energy day by day – if you let them.

Worse, the needy person will not feel bad about using you in this way, *and* that person will make you feel terrible if you are not able to help them (or don't feel like it, are tired, busy, sick, etc.).

It is not easy to break away from an emotionally needy person, especially if you have been their crutch for a long time.

To end a needy relationship, it could mean a total break. If that is necessary, it might be difficult at first, but be assured that:

(1) the person *will* attempt to make you feel guilty, possibly in a number of ways, including blaming you, and

(2) needy people always find another victim to fulfill their needs.

When this happens, remember you cannot give them your joy. You cannot let them make their problems *your* problems.

Sometimes we must think like a psychologist and listen with genuine interest and concern but at the same time, realize we cannot fix the problem. Remember we are all responsible for the decisions we have made.

Find the Blessing

We can be there for others *and* bring blessings into our life. Sometimes it is a matter of working to reestablish a level of respect for ourselves.

When we let another person totally control us, when we feel miserable and trapped, that needy person has lost all respect for us and our feelings. It may take some work, but set your ground rules and stick to them.

Regain your respect, and regain your joy.

The Curse of being a Martyr.

By definition, a martyr is *a person who endures great suffering for a cause.*

Many of us find great personal joy and satisfaction in doing for others. Truly, it is a blessing to be able to help others.

Help could be something as small as a kind word or deed at just the right moment or could be as great as major financial assistance. There are many ways to help others.

The key word here is "help" as opposed to "taking them to raise" *(meaning the person has moved into your emotional space and is taking advantage of your good nature).*

Emotionally needy people of all types look for martyrs. Martyrs will give up their own peace of mind, interests, time, and money to help those who appear to be in need. This can become a serious problem if the needy person is in that state because of consistently making bad decisions.

Sometimes the needy people are husbands and children. Family members can become so dependent that the wife/mother/daughter loses all sense of self.

Employers can be another source of martyr-making as they ask workers to give up their family or free time (great suffering) for the sake of the company's bottom line (the cause).

Find the Blessing

If you seem to be living your life only for others and are frequently unhappy, find a way to change it. You probably need to take some time by yourself to sort things out.

If there is no way to break from the needy person (an employer, for example), do something enjoyable for yourself.

It could be something small: read a good book, take a walk, shop for something you want rather than need, meet a friend for coffee and fun conversation – whatever gives you peace and blesses *your* life.

Just because you agreed to help someone does not mean you are not also entitled to blessings. Also, it is much easier to do things you *must* do if you also do things you *like* to do. Don't lose your joy.

We mourn not only for actual death
but also for the death of our dreams.

The Curse of Bitterness.

It has been said that bitterness is like drinking poison while wishing it was hurting someone else. Of course, the other person – your intended "victim" – may not even know you are drinking the poison.

All the while, the poison is hurting you and the other person is not affected in any way. If you are feeling bitterness toward someone, even if it is justified, you must find a way to let it go and have peace about your decision.

There was a time in my life when someone did me a great wrong. I was miserable over my "fate," totally broke, in great despair and very bitter.

After a period of mourning (because we mourn not only for actual death but also for the death of our dreams), I assessed my situation.

I considered all the positives – the blessings in my life. I was in good health, had a decent job, and had friends. I found a second job, and I started over.

What goes around, comes around.

I was able to move forward because I believe "what goes around, comes around."

That same advice is found in the Bible: *As ye sow, so shall ye reap (Galations 6:7).* If you are unfamiliar with that phrase, it means you will harvest whatever you plant. So if you "plant" joy and good will, that is what will return to you.

With that in mind, I told the person who hurt me that I would be fine. My final words were along the lines of, "You have made bad choices and everyone pays for their decisions.

I have peace because even though I may never know what happens, I know you will pay mightily when the time comes."

Find the Blessing

Everything did not magically get better overnight. My recovery took time, and I treasured my blessings: I had hope and people who cared about me. I had family and friends and a dog to love me, and I had faith that I could work hard and turn things around. I regained my joy.

Please don't take this to mean that all people suffering a hardship have committed some horrible act! However, we are frequently our own worst enemy, and the hardships we suffer are often directly related to our own decisions and actions (free will).

Everyone makes mistakes, but we all have the capacity to change and improve our life.

The Curse of Food and Drink.

If other things are going fairly well in our life, but we just don't seem to feel well – or if we have been diagnosed with health problems, we may need to give more thought to what we are eating.

More doctors are now promoting the benefits of a healthy diet versus the extensive side effects of most prescription medicines. However, while many people could get the same results through a change in diet or exercise, too often they would rather pop a pill and continue their destructive habits.

We want to believe our government would never let products be marketed that are detrimental to our health, but that is just not the case.

Most everyone has seen television commercials for class action suits against various pharmaceutical drugs. And just think about how long it took the government to say that smoking was *not* a good choice.

Television commercials tell us how wonderful we will feel if we consume sodas, diet drinks and caffeine-laden energy drinks, as well as a variety of chemically enhanced processed foods and snacks.

Do you drink a lot of sodas? According to numerous websites (Google *dangers of aspartame* or *dangers of diet drinks),* diet sodas in particular can have extreme side effects.

Sugar and white flour products can cause or contribute to a host of problems (including arthritis). If you do not know about food allergies, especially dairy and wheat/gluten, that is certainly worth investigating.

Find the Blessing

Don't let the wrong food and drink choices curse your life. Bless your body with the right foods. You might be surprised at your newfound energy level, and of course, that is a great way to find your joy!

If you always do things the exact same way, your results will always be exactly the same. What can you change to make a difference?

You Can Change It

If you are dealing with one of the "curses" mentioned in this chapter, take time for some deep thought as to why you might be responding the way you are.

Are you allowing yourself to be controlled by someone or by something that is causing you to be stressed, to lose your joy?

Are you missing out on the blessings that could be in your life?

Many of us reach a point where we have to make changes. When something is not working out the way you want, make a list of things that could change, even if some of the ideas are just dreams.

Brainstorming (listing everything that comes to mind) is helpful because you never know what might end up being a great idea or the right answer for your situation.

Sometimes we can get too far down into our pit of despair and can't think of anything that could help us. If that happens, find someone who will sit down with you and discuss your situation.

The right person should be someone you respect and trust, either professionally or personally, and he or she should have experienced success in life.

Most important, you must be willing to listen to this person and carefully consider changes in your life. If you continue to do the same things you have always done, nothing is going to change. The years will continue to pass and one day, you will be older than you ever thought possible and still be just as unhappy or dissatisfied with your life.

Whether you need to change your job, your field of interest, aspects of your marriage, conflicts with your child or parents, or have more personal goals such as losing weight or quitting smoking, you can be successful and find the joy you have been missing.

Remember that every day will not be perfect but as long as you are working toward your goal, you are on the road to regaining your joy.

Chapter 5
Personal Value

Personal value/respect is an often unidentified need and can be a significant contributor to stress. When we lose our "self" – our self-esteem, self-respect, self-worth, what we perceive to be our value as a human being, that brings trouble to many relationships.

By relationship, we will include romantic, friendship, business, and also parent/child. *(This is not meant to be an in-depth relationship analysis – only to mention some key points.)*

Friendly Beginnings

When a relationship begins (new job, friendship, or romance), everyone is on their best behavior. We want our best side to be seen and we want to be respected.

Over time, as we reach our comfort zones, bad habits can appear. For example, when we start a relationship (business or pleasure), we do not use bad language. We show respect for the other person, for their time and thoughts.

Sarcasm, bitterness and criticism do not exist, and we are careful not to appear needy. Perhaps we even go to great lengths to hide our imperfections.

As we become more comfortable with our new love, friend or job, some of our less than desirable qualities begin to emerge. Especially for people who need to feel superior to others, they can only hide it for so long.

Relationship Woes

Frequently, marriage problems occur when one person feels de-valued by the other. While this problem seems to be experienced more often by women, it can also be a problem for men.

How does it start? Hopefully, the marriage began with both people being equally in love with the other. Each was respectful of the other's feelings; each wanted the other to be happy. Each enjoyed doing whatever it took to make that person happy.

What happened? How did the relationship turn sour and start to fall apart?

While children are certainly a great blessing, they can also cause problems in a relationship. Suddenly there are three people (or more) in the picture and generally, the wife must take on a different role.

If the wife continues to work, it is stressful. If the wife becomes a stay-at-home mom, there may be additional stress with reduced family income. However, the most devastating stress can come from a husband's subconscious (or conscious) undermining of his wife's intellectual abilities and personal value. Suddenly, she may be reduced to little more than a housekeeper with benefits.

Of course, that is not saying housekeepers have no value, quite the opposite! This means only that a husband should never regard his spouse in that way. She is the same person he married because he loved and valued her as his equal. Once she no longer feels "equal," problems arise.

Note, also, that this problem can be reversed when the wife is the prime wage earner in the family. Anytime one person begins to feel "greater than" the other, problems generally follow.

Compliments & Conversation

When was the last time you complimented your spouse on something that mattered? Did you say the meal was good or you appreciated the clean laundry?

While "thank yous" are nice, they really don't qualify as a compliment. That usually comes under the heading of appreciation and could be compared to someone saying you did a nice job parking the car.

When have you complimented your spouse on something that actually made them feel good?

Everyone wants to be noticed when they are dressed nicely or do something nice for others but all of us, men and women alike, want and need to feel valued by our significant others and by people whom we respect. Sincere compliments are a verbal form of respect and reassurance in both personal and business relationships.

Spouses should make sure their loved ones know they are positive assets to the relationship. Parents should always treat children (including their adult children) with respect and encouragement.

In business, companies who treat their employees with respect have happy employees who work harder. People, including children, give what they get. If you treat others with respect, you will (most often) get it in return.

Conversation is very important in a relationship. When you first met, you probably spent hours just talking. If that important part of your relationship is missing, figure out how to get it back. Men might value conversation differently than women do, but it is an important connection that can make or break a relationship.

Remember that conversation is a two-way street. Merely talking about *your* interests (where the other person really can't participate) doesn't count!

Children Need Respect, Too

Perhaps the biggest problem of all is when children are de-valued or not respected. Sometimes the message is deliberate. Some parents have actually told their children they were not wanted, and that is a shameful thing to say to another person.

But often without realizing it, well-meaning parents send their children cues that they are not good enough, smart enough, trustworthy enough, pretty enough, thin enough, athletic enough, etc. and worst of all, that they just are not going to amount to anything.

When children are raised without respect, without feeling valued, it is no wonder that so many young people make poor life choices.

Turn It Around

Each of us, regardless of our age or station in life, needs to feel respected and valued by those who matter to us. In any situation: childhood, friendships, romance, marriage or workplace, when people feel de-valued or disrespected, when they lose their self-worth, problems arise.

If you need help thinking of compliments that matter, here is a brief list to get you started. Compliments cannot be followed with *"but I..."* or any other attempt to sing your own praises. People (even children) know when a compliment is sincere.

- *You did a great job on that!*
- *Wow, good job, I never thought about that!*
- *I admire your positive attitude!*
- *That is a great idea!*
- *You're so good at ____; what do you think about this?*
- *I love the way you ____! or I love it when you ____!*
- *You are so good at ____!*
- *Great job! or Good plan!*
- *That was so kind of you!*
- *You are really a thoughtful person!*

Also, asking for someone's opinion is flattering to most people. It gives us value to know someone is interested in what we think. Asking for an opinion does not mean you must choose that course; however, it is possible someone else (even a child) might have a viable idea. Children should always be asked for their opinion.

By being genuinely kind to others (leading by example), you can often turn around a problem situation without an actual confrontation.

CHAPTER SIX
Find Your Joy!

As you might have guessed by now, joy comes easier to some people than it does to others. Some folks have fewer large problems; some are more programmed to joy because they grew up in more joyful surroundings. However, it is possible for everyone to find joy in life.

In our search for joy, sometimes we must consciously distract ourselves from problems. The right distractions can help us relax and basically, take a mini-vacation from our every day challenges. The problems might still be there when we return, but we can meet them with a renewed, fresh outlook.

The following points are a classic example of *If it is to be, it's up to me.* Each one relates directly to things you can do to relieve your stress level and increase your joy!

❧❧

Smile often. When you smile at someone, it is difficult to stay depressed or angry.

❧❧

Don't expect every single day to be great. If every day were perfect, there would be nothing to look forward to!

❧❧

If you can't remember things, make a list. Each day, list your priorities and work toward accomplishing them. It is a joyous feeling to see your accomplishments.

Set goals. It makes you feel good when you achieve them. Even small goals are good. Have you ever added things you have already done to your "To Do" list – just so you can cross them off? That counts!

❧❧

If you are not exercising regularly, take a few minutes and do a few stretches, sit-ups or pushups. If you are just getting started, wall or table pushups are good.

Keep your arms straight and your feet together (regular pushup form) as you push against the wall or table. Most of us need to strengthen our arms!

If you cannot afford or do not want to join a gym, look for used exercise DVDs on eBay and amazon.com. Or turn on some upbeat music and dance. Taï Chi and yoga are also great for flexibility and stress relief.

In moving your body, you will feel better – maybe good enough to start working toward a regular routine. Even a small amount of exercise can boost your mood dramatically.

ಸಿ)ಲ್ಲ

Sometimes negative thoughts push their way into our minds. Without conscious efforts to stop them, those thoughts can multiply until we seem to be reliving every mistake we have ever made!

Even worse is when we think negatively about a situation with an individual (boss/spouse/child/other family member). Our attitude can quickly move from frustration to anger.

If negative thoughts begin to move in, immediately start thinking about positive things in your life or with that person. Generally, we have more good experiences than bad, so the list of positives should grow quickly.

If necessary, write down your list of positives. It is important to be in control of our feelings and not let negative thoughts take over and steal our joy!

ಸಿ)ಲ್ಲ

Laugh heartily at every opportunity. Always try to avoid people who complain. Laughing is documented as a vital step for physical healing and in treating depression.

Try to enjoy a good laugh every single day. Watch a funny movie. Look online for humor sites and funny videos. Laughter is an excellent way to quickly feel better!

Count your blessings instead of focusing on problems. Self-pity is a waste of time and is guaranteed to make you miserable. Remember that others don't enjoy being around people who whine and complain – and it really doesn't make you feel any better either!

Forget past mistakes and problems, and look at each day as a new chance for happiness. Each day, say "I choose to be happy." Even if problems arise, you *still* can choose to be happy. Once you give up your joy, it is much harder to get it back.

Practice random acts of kindness. We often feel better when we can help others. If physical or financial help is not a choice, what about sending a card or note? Email only if you must. There is nothing better than going to the mailbox and finding a letter from a friend.

Send a card with a handwritten note to someone who is feeling down or write to someone who has had an impact on your life. It will mean more to them than you could ever imagine.

Other random acts of kindness might be baking something to give to a neighbor or calling an old friend (to talk about happy things). Or invite someone to dinner. It can be a simple, inexpensive meal or perhaps the friend might enjoy contributing a dish. Watch a movie afterward and make a night of it.

Getting involved with planning a menu and preparing for company is a great distraction from your daily routine.

※

Make an *Encouragement File* and put positive things in it. The file can include thank you notes you have received, emails where a friend has said good things about you, and verbal compliments. Write the compliment on paper to put in your file.

Include a list of nice things you have done for others and inspirational poems or articles you find.

Make a list of your strengths and good qualities to put in the file. When you are having a bad day, go through your Encouragement File for instant joy!

※

Keep a *Blessings Journal* where you write down good things that happen. You can choose to record only the big things or keep a record of every good thing, regardless of how small.

On days when everything seems to be going wrong, take out your journal and read it.

Keeping a record of positive happenings will make you feel better and will help train your mind to look at life in a more positive way.

Each day, do something nice for yourself, something you truly enjoy that makes you feel good and relaxed. That could include reading, exercising, walking, window-shopping at a favorite store, singing, soaking in a bubble bath, playing an instrument, watching a favorite movie, etc.

Can't afford a vacation? Look for free or less expensive things to do in your area. Take a picnic to the park and feed the ducks. Take a camera and make pictures of everything.

Ask around or Google your town. Once you start looking, you might be very surprised at what you find!

What about an "at-home vacation!" Prepare or buy food in advance so there will be no cooking. Use disposable paper goods so there are no dishes to wash. Make a rule for no housework and no laundry during vacation time.

For kids, take road trips to explore your city; go to dollar movies or rent movies; go to a public pool, the park, and the library.

Research activities they can build or do: stamp a t-shirt, build and paint a bird house, play cards and board games, and outdoor games like badminton.

Have a *learn to sew* day or, if you like to cook, have a *learn to cook* day. Include a *learn to clean up* lesson with that one!

༄༅

When feeling stressed or troubled, close your eyes and visit a place or time in your memory that was especially pleasant. If it was a trip to the beach, remember the warm sand and the ocean breeze, the peaceful sounds of waves breaking gently over the sand, seagulls calling in the distance…you get the idea!

Or use a memory of a special or particularly fun day or enjoyable event in your life. Remember as much detail as possible as you take deep breaths and relax.

This also works as an effective sleeping aid when you need to quiet a busy mind. Simply tell yourself a favorite, uplifting story – one you already know well. That way, you can drift off to sleep smiling because you already know how the story will end!

༄༅

If disorder in your house is getting you down, totally clean one room so you can go there to relax and breathe freely. If your bedroom needs organizing, having that room clean might help you have a more relaxed sleep.

༄༅

Some people find joy and peace through physical activity or exercise. Meditation, even for just a few minutes, is also helpful in clearing the mind and relieving stressful times.

When you're feeling down, dress a little nicer than usual. For women, fix your hair and makeup, use perfume and wear jewelry. Even if you are not planning to go anywhere, you will feel better just knowing you look better.

If you *do* decide to go somewhere, you are ready! Do this even if it is a routine shopping trip. Well-dressed customers are treated better than those who do not take as much pride in their appearance, and just knowing you look nice will put a spring in your step!

If we are unable to work or are having trouble finding a job, stress levels can soar. Most people thrive on stimulation. We need to be around other people and we need to be reeded. If your life is missing that key ingredient to joy, start looking today for ways to change it.

Learn something new, possibly something that could help you in other ways. Learn a language, how to paint, how to faux finish, calligraphy, how to play an instrument, how to garden, how to keep bees, etc.

If you are not sure what would interest you, go to the library and look through the do-it-yourself section for ideas. The online site *eHow* is often helpful with step-by-step instructions on a variety of topics. Also look for clubs or interest groups in your area to find new friends with similar interests. Try www.meetup.com for groups in your area.

If you sew, you might enjoy doing something different like making doll or pet clothes. Give them away or sell on eBay or etsy.com. Etsy.com is a site where people sell handmade items. You might find great ideas there or on Pinterest.

※

Teach something you know. Many times, joy may be connected to our desire to contribute something meaningful to others. If you play an instrument, even if you are not a great player, you could offer beginner lessons. Sewing, cooking, and making crafts are other great teachable skills.

Advertise through your church or a local newspaper; craigslist.org could be a good source. There might be a nearby senior center or nursing home where residents would love something new to do.

An afterschool program for older elementary-aged children or home school groups might also be a great place for your special talents.

※

If your joy seems to be lost in loneliness, get involved in a group – maybe several groups until you find what you are seeking.

Church and civic groups offer a variety of interests. As you set out to meet new friends, remember that just as you enjoy talking with interesting people or those with a great sense of humor, so do they. People are drawn to others who are happy and laughing.

If you have experienced problems in keeping new friends, these tips might help.

Generally, people tend to avoid those who monopolize conversations. The #1 problem is people who drone on and on about every detail of their lives. If you think you might be talking too much, you probably are.

The #2 conversation stopper is people bragging about money and/or fancy vacations. Even worse is when they pretend to complain about how much things cost, a "clever" way to brag about how much they were able to spend.

A tie for the #2 spot is telling others how your child or grandchild is so gifted, ultra intelligent and precious in every way. That is guaranteed to end almost any conversation. You can show a *few* pictures (but not tons!); remember that everyone thinks their kids and grandkids are the greatest.

Health problems and personal or financial problems are also topics that no one wants to hear.

Politics and religion are topics that should be saved for other times – unless, of course, you are at a political or religious function.

Another conversation stopper is people who are always putting themselves down. If someone says you look great, say "Thanks!" instead of "Oh, I look awful today."

One more hint for conversing well: try to listen more than you talk. Too many folks are busy thinking of what they can say instead of listening to the other person.

Even if you have already done whatever they are talking about, try to let other people have their moment. Don't jump in with, "Yes, I did that two years ago but it's great you are just now finding out about it."

It is a burden to have to impress each person you meet, and honestly, no one enjoys listening to someone who is a classic "know it all."

Try to avoid those who are constantly passing judgment on others. They are the first to quote Matthew 7:1 *"Do not judge or you, too, shall be judged,"* when they feel someone is judging them. However, they forget that verse as they tear down other people.

If you do not feel you are an interesting person, take time to learn new things or be able to talk about current events so you will be more comfortable conversing. Get out, meet new friends, be a good listener, and find your joy!

※

It is amazing what we can learn while listening to others. Not only do we have the opportunity to learn something new, which brings us joy, but we give that person the joy of sharing their knowledge.

Sometimes we learn important information from the most unlikely sources (and sometimes from children), so it is wise to always be a good listener. You never know where you might find your joy!

※

Happiness is more difficult to find when we always look for perfection and compare ourselves with others. Don't think, "If only I had Kim's patience, could cook like Sue, and looked like Ann."

No one has *only* good qualities! We all have flaws. Concentrate on your good qualities and work on the areas where you think you might want to make improvements.

Find Your Joy

ಐಂಞ

Be kind at all times and do not sit in judgment of others. There is no way we can know or understand everything that is going on with another person.

Just because they do not choose to do something the way we would do it, that doesn't mean they are wrong. Sometimes it is best to just smile and nod! Remember we are all looking for friendly acceptance.

If we refrain from unkind, judgmental comments, we never have to worry about whether we might have offended someone. Look for opportunities to compliment others; it makes both you and the other person feel good!

"People may not remember what you actually said or did, but they will always remember how you made them feel."
~ Maya Angelou

ಐಂಞ

If someone says or does something hurtful, consider if it seems out of character before assuming they meant to hurt you. Is that behavior common for them? Could they just be having a bad day? Could you have misunderstood their intent?

Sometimes it is our perception of the action rather than the action itself. Nobody says or does exactly the right thing all the time; however, too often we expect others to overlook our mistakes while we hold them accountable for any slight mistake they make.

We should not hold others to a higher standard than we set for ourselves. Always give people the benefit of the doubt.

Generally, our friends do not deliberately try to hurt us, and it is those negatives coming up again when we simply assume that someone's intentions are bad. Also, we seem to attract problems when we *expect* to have problems. Let go of negative feelings and let your joy take over.

Remember that we all have some type of challenge going on in our life. It is how we deal with our particular problem that matters. If someone is having a bad day, it really has nothing to do with you. Do not hold it against them; give them another chance!

ಸಂಚ

Many people find joy and peace by starting the day with prayer and reading their Bible; others prefer to end their day with this comforting and relaxing routine.

If you need help starting on a more spiritual journey, visit local churches until you find the one that gives you the warmth, peace, acceptance, and joy you are seeking.

For online seekers, there are many websites to give you direction.

Ask, and it shall be given you; seek and ye shall find; knock and the door will be opened unto you. Matthew 7:7

Find Your Joy

Study Guide

The following questions go along with each chapter. They are designed to help us think more deeply about things in our life that cause stress – and help us discover how to reclaim our joy.

Take some time to answer the questions in detail and record the date of your entry. Use a separate notebook if you want.

As you grow in your joy level and look back on your answers, it will be interesting to track your progress with the dates.

Blank pages are provided at the back of the Guide for notes and tracking your progress.

Start today and find your joy!

Chapter 1

1. *What steals my joy?*

2. *What gives me joy?*

3. *How has my inner voice helped me? Or, how will I allow my inner voice to help me?*

4. *How am I kind and forgiving to myself?*

5. Do I blame others for my problems? What steps can I take to change that?

6. Do I have bitter feelings that sometimes hold me back? How can I let go of them?

7. What are the positive aspects of my life?

Chapter 2

1. *Are any of my problems related to my personal decisions/free will? List them.*

2. *Is there anyone I need to forgive? Who and why?*

3. *If I am having trouble with forgiveness, why?*

4. *Have I forced something to happen and had problems from that decision? Or, have I tried to force something to happen and realized it was a blessing when I did not get what I thought I wanted?*

5. *Am I taking responsibility for my decisions and making positive changes? If not, what can I change?*

Chapter 3

1. *Am I handling stress in a positive way? If not, where do I need to make changes?*

2. *Is sleep a problem? If so, what can I change?*

3. *Am I eating the right foods? If not, what should I change?*

4. *Do I dwell on "if only" dreams? What dreams could I turn into realistic goals? List goals and ways they could be achieved. Use the Notes pages if necessary.*

5. *What do I need vs. what do I want?*

6. *Make two lists: things that make me happy now, and things that might make me happy. Use the Notes pages at the back of the book if you need more space.*

Chapter 4

1. *Are there people in my life who are critical, bitter, emotionally needy, or who cause situations that steal my joy?*

2. *How do I allow people or situations to control my stress and joy levels?*

3. **What can I do differently to make the situation better and bring more blessings and joy into my life?**

4. **Are there other ways I can eliminate stress and bring blessings into my life when dealing with troublesome people?**

Chapter 5

1. Are there problems with personal value and respect in my life? With whom?

2. If several people are on the list, is there a pattern? What can I change to re-establish respect?

3. *Do I lead by example, giving sincere compliments to my family and friends? In what ways?*

4. *Do I look for opportunities to build up the confidence of others? How do I enrich the lives of others?*

Chapter 6

1. *Do I try to smile – do I choose to be happy? If not, am I willing to make that effort? Why or why not?*

2. *Do I set goals – short & long term? If not, buy a notebook and start today. As you keep track of your progress and success, be sure to give yourself adequate time to accomplish your goals. You can list your goals on the Notes pages that follow these questions.*

3. *Do I count my blessings? List them here.*

4. *Do I laugh often? Is it enough? How can I bring more laughter/joy into my life?*

5. *Do I make time for myself and plan things I enjoy? Is it enough?*

6. *If I need more time for myself, how can I make that happen?*

7. *Do I have an Encouragement File?*

8. **Do I practice Random Acts of Kindness? How?**

9. **Things I would like to do or new things I would like to learn that might reduce my stress, increase my joy, and enrich my life:**

Notes

Notes

Notes

Notes

www.ingramcontent.com/pod-product-compliance
Lightning Source LLC
Chambersburg PA
CBHW071312060426
42444CB00034B/2019